Peace & Love In Surrey

debut anthology

by John Griffin

Contents

To The Bard

The centuries and sundry years
  gone by since thy nativity!
Still this imperfect globe reveres
  thine almost perfect poetry.

I sin in saying (but I will)
  the passing of centuries
has not attained thy feats of quill
  in any of thy protégés.

True, there have been poets born
  who, by their own devices, have,
with words sublime, defined the dawn,
  the perfect girl, the perfect love

and in Muse-prompted eulogies,
  have told their tales of truth and tribe,
filling verse anthologies,
  each to his word his age's scribe.

But thou, superlative Shakespeare,
  thy very name stands to define
the goal of every bard's career:
  to have his fame compared with thine.

Vain hope indeed, as if, far flung,
  there slept a Stratford unexplored,
or else an England yet unsung,
  or yet a world your pen ignored.

So Will, forgive a feeble phrase;
  'tis all this scribbler can supply:
your name alone's your highest praise,
  the star in every poet's sky.

See Below

One day a letter died
  and all the consonants
and vowels remaining cried
  with doleful resonance

and every other letter,
  yes, even B and Y
said, "None of us is better.
  We'll perish, by and by."

Much silent for their chum
  stayed C, H, U and M,
S, A and D were dumb.
  None was as sad as them.

The mighty vowel, E,
  with W and O,
said, "Here's our destiny.
  Let's utter one last 'woe'!"

The Q, Z, X and J
  rang out the passing-bell
with P, R, T and K
  and V, G, N and L

then gathered with the F
  and no one heard their cries
and all the world grew deaf
  to language's demise.

But who began it all?
  Who said words must die?
Who was the first to fall?
  I'm sorry it was I.

My original title for this poem was "The Day I Died", but, as you can see, that would have ruined the punchline.

A foolish young man asking, "Will you?"
   to the girl he has put on a tie for,
reads a famed bill of fare "that'll kill you!"
   and course after course to die for!

And the windows beside him now give her
   the skyscrapers, stack upon stack,
and she casts her eye over the river
   at a million glass eyes winking back.

And now I know why he looks worried.
   These things have been known to go wrong.
If it's too slow or maybe too hurried,
   her reply is, "So soon?" or "So long".

But the eyes of his sweetheart are meeting
   that strong, copper lady, designed
to look into the morning with greeting
   and meet with acceptance, mankind;

who still holds her torch to the ocean,
   saying Yes to the new world and old
and bestows all her grace and devotion
   to the man who gets lucky and bold.

So another new nuptial's beginning.
   The worried young man now sits tall.
The dark cocktail pianist's grinning
   a black smile - the whitest of all.

The First Thought

Now, the first man to live was called Adam:
the spouse of the very first Madam,
  who laboured in pain
  for young Abel and Cain
before wondering why she had had 'em.

"It is strange, my dear Adam", she said,
as she ate up the first loaf of bread,
  "those apples I got
  that we scoff such a lot
make me feel like I'm living, not dead."

But Adam sat crunching the crust
and said, "Eve, I am nothing but dust
  and only the dross of a
  fallen philosopher,
thrall'd by insatiable lust."

At this, the first lady arose
and the clay left a map of her toes
  and she paced all round
  looking straight at the ground
with a frown at the top of her nose.

And she thought the first thought that was thought
which the best of her children are taught:
  "It is good to conceive",
  say the daughters of Eve,
"because Adam is such a good sport."

Anything Left Handed

There is a small minority
of people, not including me,
   who do a lot of things the wrong way round;
few in number, that is true,
but one of them just might be you,
   for several of their type are quite renowned.

These are they who, out of spite,
are sinister, or far from right
   but this is not to say they live in sin;
for, "On the other hand," they say,
"left-handed is the only way.
   The left-hand side's the side that's going to win!"

In London, next to Golden Square,
is Beak Street in the West End where
   the lefties have their own left-handed store;
but if you're one of us, take heed:
do not go in unless you need
   for 'righties' are a breed whom they abhor!

I drove down there the other day.
The traffic only goes one way:
   the thoroughfare, you see, is not that wide.
Apologies to all the staff
but I just simply had to laugh:
   the left-hand shop is on the right-hand side!

Alas, the shop is no longer there. They do everything on line now.

Birthday Sweets

to Zoe on her 17th birthday

Ah, when one's only seventeen
   the Belgian Buns are fresh and doughy,
pages are blank, one's slate is clean.
   A very happy birthday, Zoe.

I wish 'twas me instead of you
   enjoying all this teenage fun.
Your whole life lies ahead of you
   (except the tiny bit you've done).

More withered grows my floral store
   the more yours blossoms, ripens, blooms.
O, woe is me, I'm thirty four!
   Decrepit, senile old age looms!

But when I was your age, young miss,
   I gamboled like a frisky fawn
and reddened the metropolis
   till night itself was red with dawn.

My good looks would provide for me
   fond glances, as they shall for you.
A thousand sweethearts sighed for me
   (well, okay, maybe one or two).

But now my frame, once full of dance,
   is full of sweets and Belgian Buns.
The air now carries no fond glance
   from naughty girls (nor even nuns).

So if an overweight has-been
   might offer one quite useful tip
to someone just turned seventeen,
   keep free from Belgian Buns your lip.

Heed this and Zoe shall become
   (as in her gender's name-index
and, to the joy of Dad and Mum)
   the ultimate in all her sex.

Proud To Be British

I'm not proud to be British!
What's so great about that?
What do we have the rest don't
apart from all the chat?
For it's words that puff our billows,
words make Jack to fly,
words that run our engines,
words the tourists buy!
I'm no racist nor bigot
but there are those I resent:
all puffed-up racist wind-bags
from John O' Groats to Kent.
They make me sick with their moaning
of "wogs" and "frogs" and "commies".
Australians don't surprise me
when they call us "whinging Pommies!"
For your British lounge-spectator
spots the mote in the foreign eye
and never will moan
of the beam in his own
for a Briton must never cry.
You may say I'm a traitor
but I don't give a damn,
cos I'm not proud to be British!
... Oh, sod it, yes I am.

No Prizes

Remember a few thousand midnights ago
  when a lover was someone you kissed and no more?
Those above-the-waist cuddles, no pressure below
  to take midnight too far adrift puberty's shore?

Remember how, gradually, innocence blurred
  and focus grew sharp on ulterior aims:
contrivance of action and posture and word
  turned child into player of dangerous games?

In the river a fly-fisher, crutch-deep in leather,
  wasting the days of his fortieth June,
forgives every fish for whom he was too clever.
  No prize to be cased in his evening saloon.

For it's lighting-up time in the deepening sky
  which is pierced by a solit'ry, silvery star.
The daylight is drained through its puncturing eye
  and we watch for remembrance of all that we are.

And man on the box at the end of the news
  saves the whale from extinction, the children from woe:
happy the amateur, pleased to amuse
  what remains from a few thousand midnights ago.

Poetic Licence Renewal Form

Name:	JOHN SIMON GRIFFIN
Gender:	MALE
Date of birth:	22-03-57
Emotional condition:	VERY FRAIL
Address for future income payments:	HEAVEN
Certificates of Publication ...	NONE
... or any hope of being published?	No
How many people like your poems?	ONE

In forty words or fewer here below
give reasons why you want your Pass renewed:

I want to keep my licence up-to-date
So I may be permitted rhymes that you'd
not normally allow and to create
more verse in which facts need not be precise
and use conceit or linguistic device.

If this Application is allowed
will you observe the rules and codes of dress
and will you wander, lonely as a cloud
yet never write of daffodils?

OH YES!

If your verse is broadcast, plays enacted
or novels published, will you still agree
to waste whole days in fancy, quite distracted
like bards have always done?

OH YES. THAT'S ME.

It just remains for you to sign hereunder
within the space provided, your initials
then, at the perforation, tear asunder
and do not touch the space for the Officials.
Then post it to us with the usual fee.
Signature in block caps:

J S G.

Crisis!

Identity theft! That's what it is!
  Someone has stolen my id!
And now I don't know if I'm mister or mizz!
  Somebody pinched me, they did!

My telly, my money, my watch and my car
  are safe where I left them before,
but my soul and my ego – where ever they are,
  they're not in my head any more!

Last evening, a burglar broke into my shed
  and discovered my cranial key
for he knew that, last night, I was out of my head,
  so he nicked all the things that were me!

"He that is robb'd," said Othello, the Moor,
  "not aware of the things that he has,
who hears not the thief stealing out through the door,
  is untroubled by all that jazz."

I wish I had had not the faintest idea
  that I had a psyche to prize.
Cos then I would spare you this verbal diarrhoea
  and all psycho-babble likewise.

But ever since Sigmund invented the ego
  and started interpreting dreams,
you and I have been mentally vacant, amigo!
  We're coming apart at the seams!

If you say, "Jack Daniels", then I should say, "bourbon";
  or "dog" if somebody says "cat".
But someone said "bride", whereupon I said, "turban",
  mistaking my wife for a hat.

My lady's a princess. I dress as a frog
  in green Kermit costume and flippers
but while this goes on, our Pavlovian dog
  tends to chew up my Freudian slippers.

Alas, I can't have normal passion with her.
  You may say I'm a bit paranoid,
'cos, there at the window, a peeping voyeur
  always watches and, yes, it is Freud.

So I think I will go on a holiday soon
  go and find myself somewhere or other.
Cos, as far as I know, I'm the man in the moon
  or, knowing my luck, I'm his mother!

Lake Without a Swan

Upon a lake there swam a swan.
A lake was what she swam upon
  and, by the side,
  a painter tried
  to reproduce her grace.
The swan, in patent agony,
said, "Mister! You are stealing me!"
  The artist heard
  the talking bird
  and terror smoothed his face.

Said artist "Do I understand
you speak the language of this land?
  You must affirm
  what I discern!
  Repeat and I'll believe you!"
The swan retorted, "Fellow, why
are you surprised to hear that I
  can speak to you?
  That's nothing new!
  Your ignorance must grieve you!

"I thought the human race knew all
regarding creatures great and small;
  the way we quest
  for mate and nest
  and how we have survived.
Why do you think I've kept so still,
allowing you to use your skill?
  I knew you were
  a painter, sir,
  the moment you arrived!

"But now, alas, I realise
you see me with an artist's eyes.
  I must request
  that now you rest
  from painting my reflection.
Had you been an amateur
I would have been quite happy, sir,
  to let you spill
  and splash your fill,
  far from your art's perfection.

"But seeing how the way your grin
has prospered there above your chin,
   I'd guess your Muse
   has heard the news:
   a masterpiece is brewing,
and I in centuries to come
will hang in gallery and home
   and never will
   I die until
   millennia ensuing.

"O, have you never understood
why He who saw that all was good
   protects the swan
   from vagabond
   and lets it live and die?
I'm not like you, my artisan.
I'm not eternal, not like man.
   Oblivion
   is so the swan
   does not pollute the sky.

"Likewise the Lord of All decrees
that beasts of burden, birds and bees
   are blest above
   the fond self-love
   that you have for your race.
You made an Image out of God
and set it in the Land of Nod:
   a thing to blame
   when in your shame
   you bear too much disgrace.

"So don't immortalise me sir.
Make of my form a shimm'ring blur,
   with greys and blues
   and other hues
   to drown my soul discreetly.
The spending of a minute's toil
creates more water with your oil
   and you can make
   this shapeless lake
   engulf my shape completely."

The artist stayed entirely still
and motionlessly sat until
  a little breeze
  blew from the trees
  and whispered through his hair.
He said, "I'll change this as you wish.
I'll scrub you out and paint some fish
  and you will be
  a memory
  that no one else will share.

"This scene will now repay my name
no salary nor living fame,
  nay, though it brings
  the wealth of kings
  when I return to ashes.
I'll call it 'Lake Without a Swan'
for here is life that must be gone.
  I'll drown it so
  someone I know
  can rest below the splashes."

At this the swan showed gratitude
that man is kind as well as shrewd.
  She flapped her wings
  and told him things
  an artist can't ignore:
that on a lake a deity
saw love she thought she'd never see
  and, by her down,
  his life's renown
  would live for ever more.

On seeing a beautiful woman, walking

It is the journey of the eye from her waist,
round hip curves to thigh and up the other side
and over breasts that, covered, seem so chaste.
It is the nature of these outlines as they glide
on skilled toes, heels raised, viewed from fore or aft,
starboard or port. Which ever way she's faced,
the street she walks can never be too wide.
It is the bend and straightening of the knee,
the not-too-over-emphatic craft
given to the sway of practised ambulation
and, most of all, her confidence and glee
in effortless perfection she has laughed
to hear herself described possessing,
seeming unaware of the fruitless fascination
of a hundred men, transfixed, including me,
desiring, fantasizing and obsessing.
Oh Lord! Oh look! Oh wow! Oh glory be!

See Above

The clouds have rolled the red carpet on high.
The brief reign of the setting moon is ending,
and high outriders' planewake streaks the sky;
their bright majestic cavalcade, impending.
O, she is coming now! The stars are faded!
The forest in anticipation, twitters!
The mountains by her glances are invaded!
The topmost office skylight window glitters!
And yet, alas, these eyes cannot for long
behold the bright perfection of her face.
If strength is beauty, nothing is more strong
Nor beauteous than Dawn's effulgent face.
   Though man may yearn to gaze upon his star
   Content must he be with her blue avatar.

Ernie's Parting

Written after Eric Morecambe's death while Ernie was still with us.

O, where in heaven's Ernie Wise?!
Where's the straight man's enterprise?
Must it die when the funny man dies
   and climbs to Blessed Mary?
O, where in heaven's 'Little Ern'?
Surely for Eric he must yearn,
if only for one final turn
   on legs 'short, fat and hairy'.

Whether at hand at Eric's ops
or with Eric's hands upon his chops,
he was one of Eric's props
   but never therefore sorry
and now 'The Tall One' 's standing by
for that Great Star Turn in the Sky
which waits for all from French and Fry
   to Smith and Jones and Laurie.

Tommy Cooper's eloquence
already warms an audience
of angeline omniscience
   and chuckling cherub crowds.
He sweats beneath his famous hat
and says, "God's got a Laundromat!
It turned my fez white, jusslikethat!"
   and laughter climbs the clouds.

Eric, looking down from there,
thinks he might see Ern somewhere
and wonders if that join of hair
   refuses still to show,
or if a crack in Ernie's heart
still weeps for how they had to part
and thus, before too long, will start
   its journey from below.

But Ernie Wise, like everyone
under the warm, sweet, mortal sun,
sprints through the only known race run
   until the last sunset.
Life is so seductive still:
it quickens us with its playbill,
its live act and its vaudeville.
   The show must go on yet.

Meanwhile, on high, the patriarchs,
   bewingéd Askey, Trinder, Marx,

enough to fill a dozen arks,
　　line up to take their fill,
and Eric waits there, half in hell,
but when in mirth the heavens yell,
"Just follow that!" he knows full well,
　　when Ern turns up, he will.

Those Scottish songs ...

Those Scottish songs, and all so far away!
They sing of bonnie lasses and the hills
they long to see again some happy day
when Spring's melt-water through the forest spills.
Love-laden ballads out of long-belled lands,
those lamentations borne of laboured brow:
they fasten and engulf the Scottish glands,
they gurgle in my gloating fondness now.
My icy love falls from me as it thaws,
produces plunge-pools in its weeping streams
and lives in nature's most delightful pause,
transparent, pure and deeper than it seems.
　　My song's on Scotland's high road; I, the low.
　　Fast is my love, my heavy flesh too slow.

Valentine's Eve

13th of Febru'ry. Cupid's forces,
  camping on east horizon hills,
preen up the wings of flying horses,
  sharpen the archers' target skills.

Squadron Leader Aphrodite
  musters all her pilots now.
Friendly bombs will fall on Blighty
  everywhere (not only Slough).

Hark to the sounds of chipping, under
  knappers' hands that hone the flak,
making the arrows fly like thunder,
  spiked with aphrodisiac.

Strings of Eros' bows are stretching.
  Strong is the tension aimed at love.
Sweet is the song of fletchers, fletching
  plumage plucked from the turtle dove.

Nightfall brings the battle omen.
  Camp fires glow in the settled calm.
Dreaming lies the strong longbowman.
  All power to his lusty arm!

O, ye, the gods of love, so splendid,
  O, thou, sightless, wingéd boy,
please let all broken hearts be mended.
  Turn sorrow's tears into morrow's joy!

Come to the modern day arena,
  you famous gods of ancient reign.
Xochipilli, Venus, Clíothna!
  Here is your chance to shine again!

Rise from your cloud-enclosed pavilions.
  Bring us some extra love, because
now we are well into the billions.
  Love is scarcer than it was.

Many, so needlessly, are lonely.
  Woman has doubts and man lacks will.
Frail heart of man needs courage only.
  Woman's heart is perfection still.

Love-struck Romeos, this is urgent.
  Muster all the nerve you can.
Your path and hers will be convergent
  if you can tell her you're her man!

Tell her an absent hour's an aeon,
  yet when she's with you, time's a blink,
hers are the hills you long to ski on
  all down the piste to pastures pink.

No better day for 'carpe diem'
  hangs on the calendar in suspense.
Too soon we reach the mausoleum.
  Too long we spend there, don't we, gents?

Florists have all the means to aid you.
  Perfume loiters in every rose.
Trust to the gods of love who made you.
  They made the senses in her nose!

See, night removes its starry cover.
  Planets and moonbeams fade away.
Into the eyes of every lover
  dawn shoots the golden beams of day.

See you next year, dear gents and ladies.
  (I'll see you - you'll see this mask.)
I must be off, once more, to Hades
  (very long story ... ... don't ask).

See! The wave of Cupid's armies
  burst from the ranks of the eastern clime!
Ladies, surrender! Love-tsunamis
  smash through the bonds of tide and time!

Good luck to you whose hearts are heaving!
  Best luck to you who pant and pine!
May this battle be your achieving
  ecstasy with your Valentine!

The Colour of my Heart

Febru-erry
brings the berry.
Empty hearts are fed.
Winter dwindles.
Love rekindles.
Spring's not far ahead.
The warm wind courts
a young man's thoughts
that spoil for love and loving sports.
Mon Cherie,
please smile on me.
My heart is turning red.

Valentine,
Miss Valentine,
daughter of the Saint,
I'd do my worst
if I could burst
from etiquette's restraint.
I do not jest:
I need your breast
and all your loveliness undressed.
My heart is hot
and yearns for what
makes man's heart white and faint.

In Purgat'ry
my jealousy
I try to keep unseen.
I see you meet
with indiscreet
devoted men and keen.
They take your hand
which I can't stand.
It makes my fragile heart expand
with envy spreading
through the redding,
turning it to green.

If this day
is cloudy grey
or yellow with the sun,
or blue between
the clouds that lean
on sunshine till there's none;
which ever hue,
grey, yellow, blue,
the colour of my heart is You.
This is the day
I hope you'll say
your heart and mine are one.

We started the experiment at twenty-five past nine
  on Wednesday the fourteenth of November,
the batteries were charged up, the barometer said, "fine",
  but the reading on the board, I can't remember.

It must have been quite good because the gamma count was low
  and it didn't rise that much throughout the day.
We plotted all the relevant cross-references to show
  the reaction of the alpha-delta ray.

We placed the CX45 at twenty-four degrees
  on a transverse setting, level with the sun,
we counted thirteen oscillations, made a note of these
  and adjusted all the dials to six point one.

We tried the "Roeburg" method at a tilt of three point eight,
  but in doing so we blew a minor fuse
so we then combined the gyros with the T6 to create
  a practical replacement we could use.

The outcome was quite satisfactory, I'm pleased to say.
  The Roeburg method had no further hitch:
the oscillations doubled and the alpha-delta ray
  was responsive to the gyroscopic switch.

The experiment was steady right throughout the afternoon.
  We began the second phase at ten past four,
which involved Professor Adamson's old helium balloon
  and the DPV600, as before.

The problem that I mentioned on the telephone last night
  was that Adamson forgot he was attached
and he dangled from the basket when the thing began its flight
  as the poor professor upwards was despatched.

Now we don't know where he is - maybe somewhere over Wales,
  hanging limply by the legs and upside-down.
It's a crying shame 'cause Roeburg's method hardly ever fails.
  It's a system of professional renown.

We abandoned the experiment at seven forty-two
  and put the CX45 away.
We would have carried on but there was nothing we could do
  but we'll set it up again on Saturday.

Love Story in Sonnets

HOW TO APPROACH THAT PRETTY LADY THERE?
What does one say to her? Where sleeps my wit?
There at her table sits a vacant chair
and all that's needed is go and sit!
But beauty strikes the male desiring heart
with trembling faintness, faltering his nerve;
his pluck, his poise and confidence depart
even at the moment when they most should serve!
But now she is going! O, too late to seize
the opportunity which was so fleeting.
A curse upon this fire that can so freeze
the limbs of passion even in their heating!
   See, how beautifully she walks away
   and leaves me now to mourn the unseized day.

A MILLIONAIRE FOR YOU AND NOTHING MORE?
I think you've priced your beauty way too low!
Why, every smile you breathe would render poor
both richest man and Ordinary Joe.
Have you not seen the values rich men hold?
They cherish ambition, loveless and cruel,
which tenders beauty as it tenders gold,
coining base lucre from the sweetest jewel.
O, let your man be one who sees his prize
as you who illuminates his darkest hour
and then you'll be as happy as your eyes,
and that's the sort that can't be bought with power.
   A million's soon squandered but a heart of trust
   is worth even your beauty, though only just.

FAIR SIREN, I'D COMMIT A MONSTROUS CRIME
were I to brave you with my brutish reach.
We're at two extremities of lovers' prime,
at facing ends of the bay's curving beach,
but siren, I have dreamed of one small 'yes'
from two sweet eyes which have eclipsed my sun.
Words can't tell nor poetry express
nor music sing of what your eyes have done!
No treasure from the richest ocean buys
back one flicker from my youth now spent,
so freeze me with those day-eclipsing eyes
and I'll be an ice-man till the years repent!
   O, gentle gem, forgive these dreams of mine.
   Thoughts fly blissward from vistas this divine!

LOVE, YOU WOULD KNOW YOURSELF FROM YOUR REFLECTION
if you could see yourself with these, my eyes,
and complex would not crimson your complexion
nor bow your beauty's blushes from the skies.
Only the looking-glass you beautify
could give you confidence in what I see,
but mirrors, which are more discreet than I,
keep confidence from your discovery.
For if you saw your beauty as it is,
your love would crown a more bejeweled bearer.
One worthier than I would call you his.
Thus I am blest you think yourself no fairer.
    And I am glad your lovely eyes incline
    not to your mirror's vision, but to mine.

IF PERFECT WOMAN WERE TO MEET MAN'S GAZE
(saving Your Gracious Presence, Mary Mild),
what would she be like? Why, she would craze
his sense and turn his timid tameness wild.
Her soul more sweetly than Ravel would sing.
Her heart would make all hearts around her leap.
Her mind would know the gist of everything.
Her figure would make supermodels weep.
And Perfect Woman's walk would win more Wows
than any scaffold ever could rehearse;
if men were short of passion, she would rouse
the dullest celibates to reams of verse.
    And yet, perfection to the nth degree,
    would spoil with envy if it chanced on thee.

THE MUSE POSSESSES ONE IN EVERY AGE
who speaks in tones so tuneful to the ear
that someone such as I must stain his page
with all-unworthy words for you to hear.
Not Terpsichore herself did ever speak
to love-enraptured bards in ancient times
with more rhapsodic sound nor more mystique
than those of yours that languish in these rhymes.
You think this music beautiful, but I
have barely botched a tune more sweetly sung
by your sweet voice that can electrify
my eager ears with one tang of your tongue.
    Words never were as joyful nor so true
    as these that owe their origin from you.

THE WORLD MAY THINK THE SUN'S ABOVE THE GROUND.
The hour grows late from Leningrad to Leicester.
To me, however, night is still around
while she is sleeping her mid-day siesta.
But now some sense of day alerts her eyes
and all my dullness gets prepared to flee,
for, lo, I see her flick'ring eyelids rise
and those rich jewels inside them light on me.
Now are the edges of her lips up-curled
like petals reaching to the warming air
and, O, what lustre now ignites my world!
No smiling face was ever made so fair!
   No lady makes compare in all the Earth
   and when she wakes, she shows the world its worth.

NOT DIAMONDS NOR EXOTIC EASTERN JEWELS,
nor rubies forgéd in the tropic heat,
nor any gems upon which mankind drools
can match these ten small toes upon thy feet!
Gold ingots have I held that cost the earth,
pregnant of their promise of rich bliss,
yet even these held very little worth
compared with this thy foot which now I kiss.
Let other wights enjoy a woman's breast;
let other men suck pleasure from the teat
and yet still others, let them have the rest
and leave me but the ankles and the feet.
   Yea, let the world have jewels for its desire,
   but thy sweet tootsies are my world entire!

TILL NOW I NEVER UNDERSTOOD A WORD
the songwriters and bards were on about.
Odes, concertos, prose, I thought I heard
with kindred ears, but no, it was without.
My mind was filled with Shakespeare, Dante, Yeats,
my eardrums flooded with Beethoven, Liszt,
Tchaikovsky, Bruckner, Bach and all the greats.
I thought I'd caught their meaning, but I'd missed.
Like painters who can animate mere oil
and make one canvas speak to every age,
so music soars to heaven from the soil
and poets' seed grows pregnant on the page.
   But music, paintings, poems, everything:
   "till there was you", I never heard them sing.

OFTEN I'VE HEARD THE GENTLE GENDER MOAN
that men are all the same and want one thing.
And true it is: before his seed is sown,
man finds unsated passion gruelling.
Give him a wilderness a fortnight wide
and then his thoughts will wander from his wench
and, if he makes it to the riverside,
ask him which appetite he first must quench.
You are both wilderness and paradise.
You are Sahara and the seven seas.
Take first my love and then, as cool as ice,
I'll speak of icebergs or antipodes.
   A starved man's thoughts are narrow-minded, yet
   wide as his world when worldly wants are met.

LONG HAVE MY LABOURS KEPT ME FROM YOUR ARMS,
and they're not worth the absence I have known
these past few years, and now those doubts and qualms
of confidence so mountainous have grown
that I, with obstacles and traps beset,
each dusk bring home less freedom to my soul,
since soul and body are in deepening debt
to those with whom I should have squared my toll;
but if I'm to be true to this, my art,
as art itself's as true as lovers are,
my canvas, painted with a blackened heart,
must show more brightly its redeeming star:
   for labours would be purposeless and vain
   if your love's sunshine shone not through the rain.

LIE BACK, MY DARLING, THINK OF SURREY'S HILLS,
the dales of Yorkshire or the Devon moors,
the tributaries, streams, canals and rills,
the Suffolk fields, the shallow Norfolk shores.
Think of Wembley goalposts and the turf between,
of home-made crumpets topped with cheddar cheese.
Imagine the cricket on the village green
and English honey made by English bees.
Think me the North Sea heaving into Humber,
a Cornish crofter steady with his plough,
a Gloucester grower with a prize cucumber
or the Cerne Abbas Giant! He is me right now:
   blunt and primeval, but, sweetheart, have no fear.
   Lie back and think of England now, my dear.

BANISHED FROM YOUR BED, NO MORE I'LL WEEP.
Your love for me is gone and now's my cue
for cryogenic hibernation's sleep,
programmed to wake me in an age or two.
I've set the parameters to leave me be
until another girl like you grows tall.
O, she'll be wondrous and she'll number me
among the men she keeps at beck and call.
And those same limits will but recognise
only that lady I will most desire,
who has your beauty and your lovely eyes
which cool my soul yet set it so on fire.
   Yes, I will sleep till there relives your smile
    which lights the world and makes my life worth while.

CAN THERE BE MAGIC IN THE WRITTEN WORD
which this poor sonnet-writer's art can catch,
or is that thought, for me, a bit absurd?
Great pens pierce hearts that mine can barely scratch.
Lend me thy Muse, O Shakespeare and thy quill!
Strike up thy genius once more, O Joyce!
Huge-hearted Robbie, teach me how to fill
my page with spells and in a lover's voice.
See how my hopes of love begin to dwindle!
To conjure one small page is all I ask.
Her love, now cold for me, I'd fain rekindle.
I'd raise all ye dead poets for the task.
   But I suspect that spark's completely gone
    which magic needs so, sorry lads, sleep on.

WHEN ONE BEGINS TO SENSE THAT LOVE IS LEAVING,
Fear starts to grow and quickly gains his place
there by the eyes in readiness for grieving
when bootless brooks of love will flood the face.
Hope, in the day, cajoles, relieves and cheers
and lets you fool yourself all may be well.
Then, when the night grows deep, Fear reappears
and, like Iago, introduces hell.
Of late, I knew this Fear, for I had killed
the last hope I would ever have to kiss
the sweetest lady ever to have filled
the vacant heart of man with heaven's bliss!
   But, O, strange comfort: Hope took its last breath
    and now I'm brave! I fear not even Death!

SHALL I BEWARE, HENCEFORTH, THOSE ALPINE HEIGHTS?
My spirit climbs them only to descend
down to the deepest chasm where it bites
the dust made muddy by my tears' rich blend;
and only when that newly fertile valley
yields forth a harvest to restore my zeal,
may I, once more, with lighter footsteps, rally
upward to where a wounded heart may heal.
Shall I then spurn those himalayan trails
and court the gentler rolling hills of home?
Less lofty are her brows, less steep her vales,
her soil already rich in potent loam.
   These level paths more safely do compare,
   but Everest still tempts my folly there.

THE ROAD FROM JOY TO MISERABLE GLOOM
is one with which I'm very well acquainted.
I know all its hotels, nay, every room
and all its churches, garlanded and sainted.
Hire me for the trip! I know the way:
a broad, tail-winded, downhill, one-way street.
I'll book you into places you can stay
and I've researched the joints where you can eat.
My own descent was slow, but you can zoom.
The outer-lane expressway takes you past.
Before the gloaming we'll arrive in Gloom,
where, like the tropics, nightfall follows fast.
   Another will return you - not this poet.
   I'm told there's some way back, but I don't know it.

IS THIS THAT TREE WHOSE UPPER BRANCHES SWAYED
lighter than vapour in the summer sky
and even cooled the cloud-tops with its shade,
saluting heaven which was so close by?
Are these the budding twigs that drank the cloud
before a single drop of rain did plummet?
And are these leaves the same as those that ploughed
gentle white furrows in the summer's summit?
If so, then Autumn's cruelty has excelled
to poison so such healthy happiness,
for beauty that by heaven is expelled
can never more enjoy the clouds' caress.
   O, that such desolation might pass by,
   but fallen love still lives and will not die.

My New World

I'll tell myself it isn't true
  and, in my fantasies, shall live,
and I will patch my world anew
  and all things will be mine to give,

and from my sighs I'll make the breeze,
  my high hopes will become the skies,
I'll fashion, from these tears, the seas
  and sunshine from my scalding eyes.

All locked-up hearts - I'll set them free
  to frolic in my foaming tide
and in this Eden, she will be
  my love, my sweetheart and my bride.

This broken heart, which dreams may mend,
  though heavy still, shall sink no more.
Its gravity will seal its end:
  to form my planet's molten core.

And though Jerusalem may dip
  to lift the real world heaven-high
I'll watch it as a distant ship
  on my horizon, passing by.

Though Judgment may allow me through
  to heaven's realm, I'll let it go.
Though she'll be there among the Few,
  I'll tell myself it isn't so.

Autumn Ode

The rusting trees are packed in cotton wool.
The green of summer yields to red and gold.
The car parks in the villages are full.
The oldest stories wait to be retold.
Girls in gloves and scarves are feeling cosy.
Every young man knows this is the chance
to ripen, like a swollen plum, his nerve
and pluck one lady to the harvest dance,
sweep her with vigour till her face is rosy,
charm her ears till he wins what he knows he
does not, in all honesty, deserve.

The birds and woodland creatures gather food
as the connoisseur his winery
for autumn's plenty shall itself denude
the trees of all their golden finery:
the time of mellow fruitfulness and mists
surrenders, all too soon, to winter's chill
and old leaves, of a sudden, reappear
with tales for folks to make their babes be still.
Once more they'll say that Santa Claus exists;
their children will address the Christmas lists
and Jesus Christ be born again this year.

O, that the birds who now depart this isle
would take with them my empty memories
or that the wind would carry back her smile
that shielded so my heart from injuries;
but now the swallows gather and prepare
to leave all dearth behind and far below
and fly to happier lands across the sea
where warmer and more joyful breezes blow.
Farewell then lovers! May your winds be fair!
Fly from my sad world and my heart's despair
which, like the leaves, I wish would fall from me.

OK then, Stephen

"Write a poem in ottava rima on the subject of halitosis."
Stephen Fry, as Donald Trefusis. (Paperweight)

The dentist: it is normal to resist
his needle, his exploring hands, his bill
but with your tongue, please lick your right hand's wrist,
leave it to dry (in two minutes it will)
then smell it and you'll understand the gist
of why it's wise to dare the dentist's drill.
  A good dentist can turn into sweet roses
  that rank unpleasant thing called halitosis.

O, conquer it, this orthodontal fear!
Your dentist rightly earns his laurel wreath.
He'll help those pongy pantings disappear.
No more will you be reeking from your teeth
those dragon-draughts into the atmosphere
but breathing out the air the mountains breathe,
  no more your cherished company repelling,
  but "breath perfum'd that breedeth love by smelling".

Mine'sh a Double!

On a cold, rainy morning at quarter to two
a man staggers home, cosh he'sh had quite a few,
and he looksh for his key that will unlog the door
wish he opens then closhesh, then fallsh on the floor.
With a great deal of effort, he gets to his feet
but a horrible sight turns him white as a sheet.
There are two ghastly monsters intent on his life
and both are ferocious and both are the wife.

Clerihews 2007

A clerihew is a whimsical, four-line biographical poem invented by Edmund Clerihew Bentley. The lines are comically irregular in length, and the rhymes, often contrived, are structured AABB. I, and many other poets, use them to eulogise people who have recently died. Therefore there can be a danger of disrespect. I hope you will see that I mean none.

(February 8th)
Anna Nicole Smith
mimicked the Marilyn myth,
and married an aged millionaire.
"What a pair!"

(April 23rd)
Boris Yeltsin
Snow that melts in
Russia in the spring
reveals everything.

(April 27th)
Mstislav Rostropovich
interpreted Shostakovich
among many fellows
who composed for cellos.

(July 30th)
Bergman, Ingmar
rook, knight and king are
splendid when the game begins,
but Death, in the end, always wins.

(September 6th)
Luciano Pavarotti
joins **Gian-Carlo Menotti**
who died seven months prior
to prepare the choir.

(November 30th)
Evel Knievel
People who don't grieve'll
wonder what all the fuss is
over ravines and buses.

Know
why
I
show

my kin
and kind
my mind
within

the lit'ry
artifice
of all this
poetry.

It is because
my intellect
has much respect
for what it was.

That explanation's
one of many more
which, with metaphor,
I'll ask your patience.

Another reason is
that this scribbling wally
might whitewash his folly
and be flattered it's his.

Another's to be admired
merely for being a poet,
which would be nice, although it
is seldom in life acquired.

But why did our best creators,
Van Gogh, for example or Burns,
choose to adorn a world that spurns
its living love from all status?

For, to each of them all, there's a host
of unsung, unpublished, undisplayed,
oblivion-bound creators laid
to dust without one surviving boast.

Why? Can it be they really loved their race
so much that they committed all their days
to their art, in the hope that human ways,
thereby, would lead to gratitude or Grace?

There must be more than self-exultant passion
goading the drudging artist piece after piece.
When the daemon's with him, he cannot cease
till his work is done, despite cash or fashion.

He can't explain any more than the mountaineer
who says he must climb Everest because it's there
or they that seek gold purely because gold is rare
or they who for a death-doomed cause will volunteer.

Had I desired wealth, I might have chosen
a more marketable medium than
verse, for which the sharp appetite of man
is unready; that of woman, frozen.

I might have practiced sit-coms and laughed
for recycled bawdy and dumb show
or worse, the tabloid rag-trade below
everything: rags to riches, through craft.

A gift can make a lot of cash
for middle-men, while the giver
and his god's sold down the river,
his best creations labeled trash.

Anyway, one day he'll die,
leaving all his works behind
for future research to find
and, friends, for me, that is why.

That's why it's verse I choose.
It's worth my midnight sweat
and all invention yet
brought by the sleepless Muse.

One final reason
is for those alive
who shall survive
my life's brief season:

you must not grieve
because if I'm
true to my time,
I do believe

when time has
turned my fresh,
mortal flesh
as well as

my quill
to dust,
I trust
time will

be
true
to
me

.

(January 11th)
Sports presenter, **David Vine**
Surfaces of steep alpine
or absolutely level baize-on-slate
make absolutely zero odds to Fate.

(May 31st)
Daniel Patrick Carroll
"La Rue" in his apparel.
Eponymous Dolly, the rôle's first man!
Hello Dolly. Goodbye Dan.

(July 25th)
Farewell, **Harry Patch**
The last of that Great Batch
now joins the millions slain for naught
in wars he said should not be fought.

(July 31st)
Robson, Sir Bobby
worked hard for our hobby.
No hand of demigod prevents
his accolade, World Champ of Gents.

(October 18th)
Sir Ludovic Kennedy
Here's a brief threnody
for his Panoramic breath
which could not abolish death.

(October 8th)
Cricket umpire, **David Shepherd**
Though many a scorebook is peppered
with dotballs, fours and partnerships,
no more those little Nelson skips.

The concert violinist played a masterful finalé.
  That cat made Menuhin sound like a scraper!
The bovine lunar satellite was pure Salvador Dali
  and a spaniel barked amusement at this caper.

But most surreal of all was when a screen celebrity
  (Jude Law, Brad Pitt or maybe Mr Clooney)
decided to elope and wed a piece of cutlery!
  He ran off with a coffee spoon, the loony!

Sir Humphrey the Fragile, fatigued with his mission,
  sat down to recover his breath,
but he chose to recline on a shaky partition,
  from which he soon fell to his death.

The King's Royal Equine Physicians arrived
  (they were KREP with their medical kits).
Neither they nor their knights could get Humphrey revived.
  The poor fellow had fallen to bits.

Now, the moral of this tragic story is this:
  never perch on a wobbly wall.
You can sit on the fence if you're LibDem or Swiss,
  but if not, you are certain to fall.

Don't call the King's Men. They will just marinade you!
  They're all just a bunch of gourmets.
And for goodness' sake don't expect horses to aid you!
  They're rare among doctors these days.

Welcome to the Twittersphere

"And gathering swallows twitter in the skies."
John Keats. To Autumn.

See the timeline we're displayed on
  moving on a maker's dream.
We're such stuff as dreams are made on:
  ripplets in the data stream.
We're the twitterers of Twitter,
some of us unfit, some fitter,
some will groan while others glitter.
  We can be, or simply seem.

All you need is one computer,
  laptop, smart-phone, Apple Mac,
PC with a broadband router
  (no need to be geek or hack).
Mercury was not as fleet as
this, no, nor the fastest cheetahs!
What on Earth could be as sweet as
  sent love coming quickly back?

Type three w's, a dot,
  then twitter-dot-com in the bar.
Do the prompts and fill in what
  you want regarding who you are.
Post your mug-shot if you're pretty.
If you're not, put something witty
or a picture of your city –
  this will be your avatar.

Now say "hi" to all the planet.
  Chat with all (and all for free!).
Tweet with Justin, John and Janet.
  Follow Score_Cast (yes, that's me :)
Follow everyone I follow.
All are lovely, none is hollow.
Here's the Temple of Apollo,
  worldwide now, from sea to sea!

All our words are here for ever,
  moving down through time and space.
Someone very very clever
  made this ark for every race.
He, @Jack, the great inventor,
made this stage for us to enter.
I may never reach the centre
  but at least I have a place.

How else would you now be reading
  verse that someone such as I
could never get a single bleeding
  publisher to even try?!
They all treat my stuff like litter.
Poo to them! But I'm not bitter.
I have tweets that I can twitter
  as in Keats' autumnal sky.

We're his gathering autumn swallows.
  We're his mourning river-gnats,
tweeting dreams and watching 'follows'
  growing on our twitter-stats.
Parent, child or baby-sitter,
here's your friendly thought-transmitter.
Tweet your dreams and see how Twitter
  turns them to a hundred @s.

How can this be aught but noble?
  How can this be thought of ill?
Now our words are wide and global:
  Asia, Oz, The States, Brazil!
Some say Twitter's an illusion,
friendship, but a false conclusion!
I can settle such confusion.
  I and many millions will!

All my Twitterpals are living,
  breathing souls who comprehend
the benefits of friendship, giving
  love (which I can recommend).
Some will moan, some others titter,
some hold fast while others flitter:
each one I have met on Twitter
  I consider as a friend.

"I am going to have a pizza."
  Even if that's all you say,
friendliness in every tweet's a
  little strand of life at play.
Whether trite or esoteric,
clever, clueless, clowning, cleric,
literary or numeric,
  words are never cast astray.
Whether wholesome or hysteric,
whether homely or Homeric,
here's a brave new Twitterspheric
  world where love can win the day!

The Black Guard

The man in black stands resolutely on a field of war.
The enemy engulfs him with a belly-curdling roar
but still he stands, the solit'ry upholder of the law
  and does the thing he knows he has to do.

A man he is, in every sense, like Kipling's definition:
who keeps his head when all about protest at his decision.
Though they may shout and ridicule while questioning his vision,
  he does the thing he knows he has to do.

Few friends he has on Saturdays when out he steps at three.
No man is more courageous than the football referee.
In every match, he's always fair though some would not agree
  for he ignores what they want him to do.

He's armed with just a book, a watch, a whistle and a ball
and two flag-bearers, timid, thin and usually quite small
who, luckily for them, are not much use if there's a brawl
  when referees must do what they must do.

It is Wembley, World Cup, extra-time in 1966.
Geoff Hurst receives the ball from Alan Ball. He turns and kicks.
It hits the bar, drops down, but has it passed between the sticks?
  And now the ref is not sure what to do.

He runs to meet his linesman, who has one important rôle.
The verdict favours England. Now the Germans lose control,
and even now they quibble, but, *of course* it was a goal!
  We knew the ref was right and still we do!

The ref is also useful as the scapegoat for the losers:
"Three penalties we should have had! How could the man refusers?!"
And ladies, close your ears if you should pass the local boozers
  when they say what the ref should go and do.

What sort of man would do all this without a thought of shame?
Why does he do it? Can't be money. Can't be lust for fame.
He will say it's just because he loves the blessed game
  and doing what he knows he has to do.

At last the season ends and all the honours have been won.
The glamour-seeking champions are lapping up the sun
while the ref is in the garden, having simple, quiet fun
and doing only what he wants to do

Politics!

Politty politty politty politics!
   Politty politics! Donkey hind legs!
Beat round the bush with a bundle of fiddlesticks,
   blue in the face with our chickens and eggs!

"You're not going to catch me with questions like that."
   "The people want labour. We're going on strike."
"I'd rather not answer. I'd much rather chat
   about new manifestos the voters will like."

"The tax-payer grieves at the plummeting pound."
   Rhubarb and rabbit! Codswallop and tosh!
"Parliament Square is where statesmen are found."
   Nonsense, trash, tommyrot, twaddle and bosh!

Politty politics, talkative politics.
   "Blame the Prime Minster. Things are not fair."
Ill-chosen cabinets only a wally picks.
   Cabinets empty and cupboards are bare.

"Let's throw a party - a bloody great beano!
   Invite all the workers whose collars are blue!"
Blue is the colour and red is the vino
   and gate-crashing loonies have done up the do!

Blame the P.M., the P.M. blames the press,
   read throughout Britain and red in the face.
Stress-ridden editor alters the stress,
   saving disgrace in the loftier place.

Nevertheless we cry, "Long live Democracy!"
   (Poverty-moralists voting for bums.
The wealthy minority, dumb aristocracy
   don't hear the wisdom that comes from the slums.)

Political systems. Why do we ignore them?
   Because it is best to continue in doubt.
Government of them and by them and for them:
   the Gettysburg nonsense we can't do without.

To The Spider

"I'm truly sorry man's dominion
has broken nature's social union
and justifies that ill opinion
                    that makes thee startle
at me, thy poor earth-borne companion
                    and fellow mortal."   Robert Burns. To a Mouse.

Black haired, quick, black-legged, black-kneed,[1]
  Octopedal, multi-eyed,[2]
little grid-spinning arachnid,
  so unfavourably spied,
run for cover lest my brother,
all big-booted and roughshod,
or some Overman[3] or other
  pulls his rank to play the god.

 Never bigger than a kitten,
  though more numerous of leg;
never bigger here in Britain
  than the average breakfast egg,
human beast will flush and flatten
  with his papers, brooms and books
and with myth so misbegotten,
  doom your young life by your looks.

And this coward here stands guilty
  of recoiling from your glance,
but he won't accept his frailty
  so he'll travel back, in trance,
to the time of that first error
  when his uncorrupted heart
was infected with the terror
  that keeps you and he apart.

For his hypnotist is asking
  him to use his adult thoughts
on his memory, unmasking
  what the childish mind reports
as a mesmerising visage
  with a dark, nightmare surround

---

[1] *black-kneed* — I realise spiders don't have knees necessarily. I just needed a barely acceptable rhyme for "arachnid".
[2] *multi-eyed* — A spider's visual acuity is poor, so nature compensates by providing the creature with more eyes, sometimes up to twelve!
[3] *Overman* — The Nietzschean "Übermensch", more commonly translated as 'Superman'. Overman is not only a more accurate translation, it also avoids unnecessary (and perhaps comic) confusion.

which began a harmless image
   where no threat should have been found.

I am five and Ian Fleming's
   Dr. No takes movie shape
and my fellow life-lorn lemmings
   rush to see it and escape
from their unrenowned, dejected,
   diabolic world of noise
to a two-hour disaffected
   realm of resurrected joys.

Five years old, to see such daring,
   such finesse of brawn and brain:
Bond is winning fights and baring
   girls and leaving villains slain.
O, such confidence in taking
   everything he wants to take!
Then I see the hero waking
   and I feel the audience quake.

Even James Bond cannot govern
   such a dreadful, deadly threat!
Now the face of 0-0-7
   is a leaking dyke of sweat.
Someone whispers, "It's the spider!
   Ugh! It's crawling up the sheet!"
and my gawp grows ever wider
   as I fear what it might eat!

Any weapon Bond can master,
   any challenge he will scoff.
Crime is fast but James is faster:
   vodka, kill, kiss, kip and off!
Blackjack tables he will bluff in
   and the drinks he'll never stir
and the hotels he will love in
   are the best there ever were.

Every theory and aesthetic,
   any vintner's taste and tint,
every escapade athletic,
   though lampooned by Our Man Flint[4]
are at Bond's benign disposal
   and it's Bond we still prefer,
for his deeds with death and damsel
   are the best there ever were.

Any despot he could handle.
   O, he could have freed the Kurds
and you cannot hold a candle

Our Man Flint — A James Bond spoof, featuring James Coburn.

to his ways of bedding birds.
Give him danger he will love it
   but one spider makes him seem
scarcely braver than Miss Muffet:
   all the scare (without the scream).

The apprentice[5] sees, minutely,
   the revulsion at the view
as the tutor resolutely
   clubs the creature with his shoe.
James may know the names of grocers
   from Helsinki to Milan
but he doesn't know lycosas[6]
   very rarely relish man.

Be it film or fact, the media's
   one-sided story blooms
while pristine encyclopædias
   withhold their wise perfumes
from the snouts that might get wind of
   good and evil and beyond
and find faults few comprehend of
   in the licensed acts of Bond.

Peacetime brings the phantom rivals
   only made-up heroes meet.
People feel at peace with evils
   simple virtues can defeat.
Brosnan, Lazenby and Niven,[7]
   Dalton, Moore, Craig, Connery
are summarily forgiven.
   Bond is fond in memory.

O, he never knew the horrors
   he was planting in the hearts
of a million little terrors
   who now suffer fits and starts
as full-grown arachnophobic
   adults, loose of rationale
when a harmless tegenaric[8]
   scuttles blindly down a wall.

When my "best friend", Rex or Rover
   bounds, I'll merely laugh his name,
yet the party's all but over

---

[5] *apprentice* — I think every young man fancied himself the successor to Mr Bond.
[6] *lycosas* — The lycosa tarantula spider, witnessed in Dr. No. The correct plural is probably lycosi.
[7] *Niven* — Yes, the original Casino Royale was only another Bond spoof, featuring David Niven but the rhyme was irresistible.
[8] *tegenaric* — Tegenaria gigantea: the common house-spider.

for poor Teg[9] who does the same.
If a fly visits my garret
  maybe freighted with disease,
it is you, healthy fly-ferret
  who will make me ill-at-ease.

I am chilled down to the marrow
  at the friend who hunts the pest
when the cat that kills the sparrow
  finds me at my tenderest.
Down through folklore you've been tortured
  and in ode you don't belong
while the bird who robs the orchard
  dwells in poetry and song.

Greek Athena, when embittered[10]
  and of victory bereft,
left the Lydian heavens littered
  with Arachne's finer weft.
Ancient goddesses and heroes
  pass their woes and foes and fuss
down through emperors and pharaohs
  to inferiors like us.

We are quick to learn of evil.
  Flesh is easy to offend.
We will contemplate a devil
  when we should perceive a friend.
It takes years of self-persuasion
  to unlearn the wrongs of old
and still, on the odd occasion,
  one arachnid turns me cold.

Psychoanalysts conjecture
  that the vague exotica
and the fearful architecture
  of the semblant swastika
and the sinister appearance
  of the mesmerising frame
and the spinster perseverance
  of the spider are to blame.

Hypnotherapists have told me
  I've an unpurged, ancient fear
and this phobia will hold me

Teg — My whimsical name for the house-spider. Shakespeare does similarly with his fox in Venus and Adonis ('poor Wat').

  Greek Athena ... — This is a truncation of the Arachne myth. The goddess lost to the mortal in a spinning duel and, in fury, turned her into a cosmic spider, commemorated by one of the constellations. The story, according to Robert Graves, has its origin in a trade conflict between Athens and the town of Lydia, noted for its silk-weaving industry. The Athenian competitors eventually cornered the market.

till I've tranced back to the year
of some misadventure, rooted
   in my childhood, linking pain
to a spider, convoluted
   like a cobweb in the brain.

It's the cinematic notions
   I suspect, though, were the cause.
Didn't film-buffs fear the oceans
   after Moby Dick and Jaws?
Yes, it seems a showbiz trauma's
   where my horror sprouted from,
cast abroad by dint of dramas
   then by Harry, Dick and Tom.

There are theories, endless theories,
   every expert has his view
and a documentary series
   had an episode on you;
but not one white-haired professor
   can explain to my content
why your deadliest aggressor
   holds this hate which I lament.

You're a genius in nature
   with your ginning-spinning art
and for all his sericulture,[11]
   man is nowhere near as smart.
I have seen the way you capture
   like a fisherman[12] your prey
and have studied you with rapture
   at the silky dawn of day.

When the hoar frost on the bindings,
   on the beams and spokes and seams,
and the bridges and the windings
   of your latticed webbing gleams,
there's a god who says, "Exquisite!
   I must show this to the sun!"
And then daybreak's Midas visit
   turns to gold all you have done.

Five years young I knew your beauty
   but my psyche had been conned.
I was sure it was my duty
   to become a thing like Bond.
But although I learned the accent,[13]
   mine were years of Save-the-Whale,

---

[11] *sericulture* – silk weaving.
[12] *like a fisherman* – Some spiders literally fish for insects, dangling their silk threads from above.
[13] *But although I learned the accent* – the preceding line (in which I have practised a passable Sean Connery) is better spoken aloud and, therefore, informs the line following.

Ban-the-Bomb, bullfight and fox-hunt
  and the female's rights are male.

So the New Man slew old dirty
  here inside this fashioned frame
and when I grew to thirty,
  I was tethered, trained and tame.
I had learned to tell man's folly
  and the bad guy from the good
and the smart-arse from the wally
  and the wiles of Hollywood.

And I realised our judgment
  is distorted if we heed
not the words on wisdom's parchment
  (sometimes difficult to read),
but the pat presuppositions
  on the screen and in the press,
obfuscated with omissions
  and the bluff one-sided stress.

Lies were what truth took its shape from
  and escapism became
like a prison to escape from:
  full of doom and crime and flame,
actors stabbing, kicking, shooting,
  murders hot and serial;
art's ambrosia transmuting
  back to raw material.

So I turned my nose from violence
  to the bravest smell of all
and in learning's scented silence,
  turned the leaves that Ayr[14] let fall
and a mouse, who might have frightened
  sullen dame[15] to climb her chair,
was absolved and mankind heightened
  by a careless ploughman's care.

Thus I took poetic word as
  truth, life's sanctity as read
and repented all my murders
  to the unborn and the dead,
be they reptile, rodent, vermin,
  be they brown or white or red,
Moslem, Methodist or Mormon,
  be they leaders, be they led,

Ayr — Robert Burns lived mostly in and around Ayr. This subtlety is lost if spoken to an audience,
ut I couldn't resist the pun.
sullen dame — from Burns' poem Tam 'O Shanter: "... oor sulky, sullen dame / gathering her brows
e gathering storm / nursing her wrath to keep it warm".

be they ignorant or witty,
  be they arrogant or meek,
unattractive, plain or pretty,
  be they powerful or weak;
and I cry to every city,
  for a moment hear me speak:
hatred's higher part is pity!
  love itself is pity's peak!

But my voice drowns in the honey
  of the do-good, half humane,
moral void that thinks me funny
  for my Creeping Thing campaign;
and, enchanted by the tasteful,
  handsome, sweet or grandiose,
draws its lifeline for the graceful,
  draws its death-mark for the gross.

'Purging beasts,' they say, 'is pitiful
  if ears can hear them howl,
for the Lord God made the beautiful
  and Satan made the foul.'
Human brains, brimful of bunkum
  and with daffodils adorned,
deem the pretty creatures welcome
  while the ugly ones are scorned.

Does your bite give people rabies?
  No, and dog bites sometimes do,
yet we grizzle loud like babies
  at the grizzly sight of you.
Well, from now on I'll indulge you
  in your alcove, niche or den
No, I never will divulge you
  to the luckless hands of men!

Understand us, welcome lodger,
  crime's a thing we love to forge,
so forgive Pierce, Sean and Roger,
  David, Daniel, Tim and George.
Bond was manhood's final pageant
  and, alas, I never grew
to a latent secret agent
  (though a gadgeteer like Q).

Here is all I know of Paradise.
  Your doom I can't condemn
to a carpet-hugging sacrifice
  for, out of Bethlehem,
came the substance of communion,
  the eternal guarantee:

if I license my companion,
  He will always suffer me.

Now the doctor snaps his fingers
  and the hypnotizee blinks
and although his terror lingers,
  he's a wiser man (he thinks);
he has seen the spring and fountain,
  though he still can't stoop to drink.
He would sooner climb a mountain
  than redeem you from the sink![16]

His, the coward's eye, cast backward,
  on psychiatrist advice,
found all recollection awkward,
  through an inscape webbed with vice.
Built on misdeed, fraud and fiction,
  his incarnate crime called "Me"
makes him scant of glad prediction
  for the virgin time to be.

But he'll never kill a spider.
  Life's a greater gift to give.
He's a different law-abider:
  his, a Licence to Let Live.
Though he'll meet with callous rival
  and a curds-and-whey showbiz,
he'll endeavour your survival.
  All your enemies are his.

Maybe he who cannot love you
  (half-blind, brittle, black and brisk)
yet may presently approve you thus:
  O, little asterisk!
Life's reminder that the spider
  stands astride the zodiac,
spinning wider still and wider,
my deceiver and my guider,
I'm your fellow planet-rider,
  an arachnophobiac.

---

redeem you from the sink — save you from being drowned in the sink, into which spiders often
tumble. They never arrive there from the pipes below — a common misconception.

Birthday Bumps for Bill Blake

Written on 28th November 2007 to commemorate the poet's 250th birthday.

O, ROSE THOU ART SICK.
Thy mind has gone berserk!
Here's med'cine. Drink it quick.
We need you back at work.

You were a bit foolhardy
to quaff a whole rum flagon.
For you: no more Bacardi!
You're going on the wagon!

BRING ME MY BOW OF BURNING GOLD.
BRING ME MY ARROWS OF DESIRE.
Alas, I'm getting far too old.
In the afternoons, I tend to tire.

They're in the drawer marked "weaponry".
You'll find my spear in there as well.
Bring them to me presently.
I need to build this citadel.

TYGER, TYGER, BURNING BRIGHT.
Who on earth set you alight?
I'll understand when now I hear,
"Put the cat out, will you, dear?"

I guess a bunch of laughing lads
wanted something to ignite.
We saw you in those Esso ads
promoting petrol! Serves you right!

Here on the boundary, keeping score,
I mark each maiden over 'M'.
Few of the players know this chore
nor how I sorely envy them,
   nor how the concentration strays
   from cricket's laws and long delays.

Have you seen this south-west sky:
its red-cheeked clouds and puffed-up breast
that, reaching Ashtead, hears the Rye,
whose soft persuasion bids it rest?
   When other pretty shires are near,
   why does it pause precisely here?

Here where Surrey's fringes skirt
at London's bustle, hemmed with green,
the motorway takes all its hurt
away to places less serene.
   Here's where cares and woes transform
   to quiet calm amid the storm.

Marking the day that Shakespeare died
who "set the teeth" that men have snarled,
St. George's flags are hoist worldwide
and here, from Milners to The Marld.
   Yet every Ashtead dweller knows:
   here be no dragons. Here's the rose.

And Ashtead's Hall remembers Peace,
though memories of war remain.
I fear man's fighting may not cease
till there are no fields left to gain.
   O, that 'Peace' graced every spar
   on all the village halls there are!

Beneath our feet, long worlds ago,
the Roman, off the beaten track,
trod the very clay we know,
found Ashtead Woods and looked not back.
   That Roman tileman's chiseled skill
   echoes in the mind's ear still.

Even now, nice people come
to Ashtead and decide to stay;
people like my Dad and Mum,
and gentle clouds at close of day
   red carpeting the damson sky.
   Again, I ask the question, why?

"Howzat?!" the leaping fielders cry -
my daydream snaps at this ado.
The umpire's finger gives reply,
which satisfies my question too,
   it points to heavens that overglide
   where Ashtead, love and peace
       reside.

If you can keep your distance when, behind you,
  a fellow motorist cannot keep his,
and with his full-beam headlight, tries to find you
  more timid than he likes to think he is;
if you can wait to change your lane with caution
  and not encroach on someone else's space,
thus favouring to each his own proportion,
  as is his right and yours with equal grace;

If speed and not expedience was your master,
  bethink you now which course would prove more brave:
to thunder down the highway to disaster
  and suffer rescuers to find your grave,
or manfully to bear the law's restriction,
  maturely to uphold the Highway Code
and reason with your own wise jurisdiction
  the safety regulations of the road;

If you commit that inadvertent bloomer
  which you are bound to, being flesh and blood,
but can admit it humbly and with humour
  though all about may swear your name is Mudd;
if you can heed the unexpected warning
  that indicates some accident nearby,
obey the limit other folk are scorning
  yet cause no queues by slowing down to pry;

If you can take the back-seat-driver's nagging,
  show patience when denied your right of way,
forgive the senior citizen his lagging,
  remembering that you'll slow down one day;
if you have read these verses acquiescing,
  or if you've only understood the gist,
yours is the forward progress worth progressing,
  and, which is more, you'll be a motorist.

Three Non-Limericks

There once was a limerick penned
with a whole extra line at the end,
but it sounded all wrong,
it was one line too long
and it failed to live up to the trend
of a verse form one mustn't extend.

There once was a four-liner written,
the first of its kind here in Britain.
It started off fine
but was missing a line.

Yet another one just didn't scan.
It was written by the very same man,
and as if that wasn't enough,
it didn't rhyme either
and was considered by all and sundry as a complete load of rubbish.

This is London

Tune: Lily Bolero

Rock-a-bye London, sleepy old town.
When the wind blows her bridges fall down.
When the world threatens island and sea,
London becomes what London can be.
This is London, singing her anthem,
on the World Service each hour of the clock,
reminding the planet that London once ran it
and will do again when cradles will rock.

This Christmas, put away the sled,
get in the car and go and look
in Surrey, north of Leatherhead
and south of Chessington and Hook.

You'll have to keep a beady eye
and slow the car down to a crawl
for if you blink as you go by,
you'll miss it. It is very small.

Malden Rushett is its name:
hardly a village, barely a mews!
Its only claim to lasting fame:
a traffic crossroad, causing queues!

But when November's final plum
drops like the dusk on longer nights,
the Borough Council's men will come
with Malden Rushett's Christmas lights.

I'd guess it takes two hundred skilled,
determined artisans to dress
each lamp post in such glory-filled
magnificence. It can't be less.

For when the job is done, behold!
Spiralled around each post there glows,
beneath each lamp of shining gold,
a string of bulbs beyond all prose!

And quite beyond comparison
are Streets of Oxford, Regent, Bond.
Not even Tony Harrison
could write an ode to correspond!

O, I was there upon the Thames
when fireworks greeted "y2k":
six barges fired their bursting gems
above Big Ben at Hogmanay.

And Piccadilly Circus thrills
(with coloured flashing sight and sound)
the eyes of Jacks and pretty Jills
and foreign Johnnies all year round.

And in the tow'ring New York skies
on Indepedence Day - good grief!
But Malden Rushett gives the eyes
a spectacle beyond belief!

Yet Malden Rushett seems quite fit.
O, such a place was Bethlehem:
a little place, not brightly lit -
its lights - I would not laugh at them!

Not dwarfed beneath a hundred tow'rs,
not blest with aught that would impress,
not busy in the early hours;
a bit like Malden Rushett, yes?

That village in the Holy Land
(till blesséd Mary's Son arose)
was unspectacular and bland
like Malden Rushett, I suppose.

This Christmas, I'll have no sleigh bells.
I'll turn my thoughts and blessings on
that place of which this story tells
twixt Leatherhead and Chessington.

Memo

Will broadcasters please show some mercy
and pronounce the word 'controversy'
for it shows linguistic poverty
to render it as 'controversy'?
You wonder why I show such anguish?
I hate to hear my language languish.

Before they arrive,
before they get to you,
prepare all the tea-churns you have.
They will weave for you.
Let them come and weave for you.

I wanna be up on the 'ill today,
I wanna be up on the 'ill.
In a number of ways and today of all days,
I wanna be up on the 'ill.

I'm entitled to go up the 'ill today,
entitled to go up the 'ill.
It's not out of spite, it's a God-given right
and I'm gonna go up on the 'ill.

The mujahideen are coming today.
The mujahideen are 'ere.
'eroic and brave and they live in a cave.
When they pass, I will give 'em a cheer.

You don't wanna go into town today,
no, you don't wanna go into town.
Today of all days, the sun nor 'is rays
will wanna go into the town.

You're entitled to go into town today,
entitled to go into town,
but, Lord, if you do, then it's curtains for you.
You do not wanna go into town.

With rugs at the ready and bended of knee
and needles and thimbles and mugs full of tea,
the mujahideen sit them down and agree
on the thing they're about to create.
Faroukh ibn Shah wants it fit for a sheikh.
Kamal says, "Okay, but it mustn't be fake."
Muhammad says, "Fine, but what ever we make,
make sure that the canvas is straight."

The mujahideen are coming, are coming.
The mujahideen are here.
They are stitching and sewing
and weaving and throwing
the shuttle and showing no fear.
The mujahideen are coming, are coming.
They're manfully smoking their drugs.

They are sewing and knitting
and nothing omitting
and all of them sitting on rugs.

"Don't mess with me," says Faroukh with a frown,
his needle-thumb leathery-weathered and brown,
"or else I will pick out the stitch of your gown
and you'll struggle to rejoin the fray.
We will come to your village and put on a show" -
(they're touring throughout the Home Counties, you know) -
"Sundays and weekdays, where ever we go,
we're as welcome as flowers in May."

The mujahideen are coming, are coming.
The mujahideen are nigh.
They're casting and threading
for wake or for wedding
in Ramsgate and Reading and Rye.
The mujahideen are coming, are coming.
They love to have dope, tea and fags.
They'll be knitting and purling
and tucking and curling
and soon be unfurling the flags.

The idiot "up on the 'ill" would say,
in his cursing, conniving and cowardly way,
"You don't wanna go into town today -
the peril down there is rife!"
But we, who are nothing if never courageous,
always find heroes completely contagious.
Great ones like this never fail to engage us
in tapestry's affluent life.

The mujahideen are coming, are coming.
Embroidery covers their laps.
They are snipping and slashing,
they're so haberdashing!
They're utterly smashing young chaps!
The mujahideen are coming, are coming.
They're here with the crescent-shape moon.
They have put down the sabre in favour of labour.
They'll be in your neighbourhood soon.

And when they arrive,
when they get to you,
let them have plenty of tea,
and let them weave for you,
and let them go.

Orange, purple and other difficult rhymes

How I have wrestled with rhymes impossible!
I mean, you try and find a rhyme for "month"!
There isn't one! And here's another - "chemist" -
unless you are a clever apophthegmist
who has a lisp and starts each story, "Wunth
upon a time" to children in a hothpital.

Here stands a pair before me now
who want to make their marriage vow.
The groom's name is an awkward colour
Orange, but his bride is duller:
Purple is her name and I
must marry them. OK, I'll try.

Mr Orange, will you take
the first bite of your wedding cake
with this your new and violet bride
and stay forever by her side?

"I will", said he and put his ring
upon her lilac finger
Then I asked the plum-faced thing
if she with him would linger.

"Will you love for evermore-and-j
oin in wedded bliss with Orange?"
"Yes, OK," said she, "this twerp'll
be a husband unto Purple.

And all the congregation knew
(for they were coloured people too)
the wedding rings were gold and silver,
and they would honeymoon in Manilva.

For those who don't know where that is
it's down in Spain quite near Cadiz
where Orange is hers and Purple's his
for better or for worse.
As colours, both are fairly brash
I'm sure that sometimes they will clash.
and with that word I now must dash
and end this stupid verse.

Three very short Christmas poems

1
There is an old geezer called Claus
with a snowy white beard on his jaws.
It's a beard made of snow
and it's dignified, though
it reveals his war wound when it thaws.

2
On Christmas day at strike of three,
before the Great Escape,
the Queen's address on BBC
is broadcast from a tape,
but Queenie doesn't make much sense
(it's really not her fault)
and yonder looms the barbed-wire fence
McQueen nor Queen can vault.

3
A fellow called Old Father Time
come Hogmanay, reaches his prime.
As a wily old seer,
he says, "Happy New Year!"
then returns to the scene of the crime.

The Lunatic

*" ... for it is profitable for thee that one of thy members should perish,
and not that thy whole body should be cast into hell."*
Matthew, 5, 29.

*"O, let me not be mad, not mad, sweet heaven,
Keep me in temper: I would not be mad."*
Shakespeare. King Lear.

Some people say I'm mad
but what gives them the right?
To them I say, "Jihad!
Get ready for a fight!

"You'll find me full of hitting:
of hitting I'll be full,
for I'll put down my knitting
and whack you with the wool!"

They mutter that I'm barking.
They say, "He's off his chump.
His spark-plugs are not sparking.
A bike without a pump."

They're always so unpleasant,
but I'll catch them together,
I'll pluck an August pheasant
and flay them with its feather!

They always have a go at me.
They think I'm such a weed.
The 10p coins they throw at me
can make my forehead bleed.

A hundredfold I owe them
a torment like Gehenna's!
With my revenge I'll show them!
I'll pelt them all with tenners!

O, I will do such things:
the terrors of the earth,
that even ancient kings
will dread my coming birth!

And lo, the full moon rises!
The one that Merlin saw.
The one the lover prizes
and lunatics adore.

The time is ripe for madness.
Romance is for the fool
who spends his days in sadness.
Let idiocy rule!

Cruel sunshine reprehends me.
Far kinder glows the moon.
My jealous heart offends me.
I'll cast it from me soon.

And free from love I'll flourish
with daisies in my hair
and daffodils will nourish
the greedy goblins there.

But, I have dreamed with Dante
in Purgatorio
where lost souls search for shantih,
above them and below.

It passeth comprehension
why they cannot find peace.
They hunger for ascension.
They long for their release.

On that invented landing,
that burning mezzanine,
it passeth understanding
why nothing is serene.

It's different up in heaven
(yes I've been there as well),
where all things are forgiven,
yes, even things from hell.

Up there I learned of mercy
where grudges don't belong.
There is no controversy
between what's right and wrong.

My wisdom is all-knowing,
so don't tell me I'm mad.
And now I must be going.
Here endeth my jihad.

My path is smooth and level
and goes beyond the Nile
where I will greet the Devil
with a kind, forgiving smile.

To the Cosmic Dancer
for Marc Bolan

Radio-raised bard of the spinning flies,
  how young you left this ever-grieving world.
The last dinosaur closed his dreaming eyes
  and summer ended. Both had grown too old.

Tolkien-talking star of the shine-machine,
  friend of the very tree your ending spelled,
Feld was your name and when your life had been,
  O, how we wished that arbour had been felled.

Its woodnymph surely must have been possessed
  or else green-envious of elven sprites,
maddened by moonshine in her leafy breast
  or giddy with the glories of the heights

or angry at the world's September hunger
  which hoards up its supplies against the time.
Which ever sin it was that caused her anger,
  another good man died in wisdom's prime.

Children we were, fantastic and aware,
  tuned to starlight and the cosmic spheres,
dreams of planets orbiting our hair,
  alas, made on the stuff that disappears.

But custom wills that comfort should be drawn
  from every tragedy, so may your tomb,
to use your rhyme, yield forth to be reborn
  your spirit, dancing from another womb.

Canoeing to Mergui

Why do the tropical countries allow this?
Back home in Britain there'd be much ado.
Let me explain my bizarre situation.
I won't be surprised if it's happened to you.

I got to Tavoy where a small cabin cruiser
was meant to be leaving at quarter to eight
for an overnight trip down the coast to Mergui.
I'd got the right day and was not running late.

Now, as it turned out, there was no cabin cruiser.
It left with the ebb tide around about noon.
The only alternatives left were as follows:
on foot, by canoe or by hot-air balloon.

To hoof the one hundred and twenty odd miles
through the swamps north of Palaw with rucksack and guide
would have slain the best part of a week I don't have,
and by hot-air balloon, well, it's never been tried.

So I'm here in this damp and small chiseled canoe
off the coast of a country most tourists avoid.
The man whose canoe this was wouldn't take cash
so my shoes are now his and I'm bloody annoyed!

Only in tropical lands would this happen.
back home in Britain, there'd be an uproar.
Some do-gooding organisation would grumble.
The powers-that-be would have me to ignore!

The guns could be heard in Surrey

North-west blew the wind from the trenches,
  the south-easterly fetcher of sounds,
which Sussex and Kent often quenches
  before it can reach the North Downs.
It must have blown hot with its hurry,
  for its gust bore the battle's brunt
and the guns could be heard in Surrey
  all the way from the Western Front.

And I fancy Leith Hill's where they uttered.
  which is Surrey's high listening post
where a clear vista, freshly uncluttered
  climbs all the way down to the coast.
And I try to imagine the worry –
  as a second skin wrapped around men –
for the guns could be heard in Surrey
  by anyone listening then.

Yes, I know all the verses of violence
  from Owen and Graves and Sassoon
but remembrance lives more in the silence
  to which we have grown so immune.
The men who fell dead in the slurry –
  the wind never carried their cries
but the guns could be heard in Surrey
  under silent Surrey skies …

… which for them would have been ordinary:
  back then there was none of our noise
and the wind through the Thames estuary
  may have carried the sounds of our boys,
but we would not have heard the furore
  nor the sacrificed flower of youth
for the guns only told of the glory
  leaving poets to tell us the truth.

They wrote with a colour and candour
  the government would not allow.
Their attempt to expose propaganda
  was as vain as it would be now.
Too stark was their vocabulary;
  too raw for the big guns to chew;
there were young guns and blushes to bury
  but we must not forget what was true.

They are no longer here to remind us.
  That great generation is gone,
but 11/11 should bind us
  in thought and in deed from now on
and in hoping for war's final flurry:
  for the last soldier ever to shoot,
and for guns evermore heard in Surrey
  to be only the guns of salute.

Wings

All the chickens on the roof
  watch a penguin in the sky
give the doubting gazers proof
  that a flightless bird can fly;

and an ostrich in the highest
  of the branches on a tree
(and who once had been the shyest),
  chirrups proudly, "Look at me!"

And the eagles and the swallows
  pace the pasture far below
with the jealousy that follows
  admiration, like a crow.

And, behold, you are the emu,
  flying effortlessly now!
To their thinking, it will seem you
  haven't ever not known how!

And the dull peacocks admire you
  and the colours of your flight.
Let the rising moon inspire you
  forward, onward into night!

Sing the song that will embolden!
  Drink the draught of air that fills!
Till the new sun and its golden
  treacle, trickles down the hills.

And one day, when you are older,
  this night's joy will be your song:
of the tail-wind on your shoulder,
  pushing, pushing you along.

And ensuing generations,
  though they flap their wings in vain,
will migrate throughout the nations
  and they'll sing your song again.

See! The whole world sings together!
  Every single creature sings
of the one who dared to feather
  at the heavens with his wings.

We could have listened to the nerds

Before our children pay the cost
and everyone we love is lost,
I have a tale to tell to you
which is important, grave and true.
   I've known it since I was a tot.
   I don't think I have lost the plot.

Somewhere another humankind
(unlike our failed experiment),
born from the dust it left behind,
lives in perpetual merriment,
   working towards a worthy end,
   richer than desire can spend.

Yes, they had their moments too;
their "one small step", their "giant leap",
but unlike us, they followed through,
flocked and followed (not like sheep)
   high to the sunlit uplands where,
   though eagles die, yet brave men dare.

Between our neighbour stars they stride.
The sky is not the limit there.
Horizons high, profound and wide
inspire the spirit everywhere.
   Their mother planet slows and tires
   but they'll live on when she expires.

In all the cosmos there will be,
of man-made objects left, but one:
a spacecraft, representing me
and you and all men 'neath the sun,
   floating to races humanoid
   far, far away across the void.

So, one day, many years ahead,
Bach will be heard in places where
no one will know the race is dead
that loved and sent his music there.
   Morse Code, whale song, wind and thunder –
   What will they make of those, I wonder.

And on another day, perhaps,
a million million aeons hence,
our waves will have traversed the gaps
to reach by chance or providence,
   the eyes of other races who

will learn from all our errors too.

Thus our extinction won't have been
in vain, for wiser worlds will learn
what their existence has to mean.
Their tide, if ebbing, then will turn,
  break the surly bonds and rise
  into the safety of their skies.

Good for them! O, if I knew
these happy folks, these souls-to-be,
I'm certain I would love them too
and fancy they would suffer me
  and my sad tale of humankind
  who died with wakeful eyes and blind.

A failed experiment of clay,
we loved our kids but were not fond
of riches that we knew would pay
for their tomorrows and beyond.
  We loved our kids but would not give
  enough to let their children live.

Instead, we lived a local lot,
of global issues made no fuss,
except when we complained of what
our countries could not do for us.
  We waited for our leaders, who
  had no idea what to do!

They thought that time was on our side,
that Earth would keep us safe from harm,
that asteroids would not collide,
that I was from the funny-farm!
  And though the threat was widely known,
  they disregarded Yellowstone.

And one day, she exhaled her breath,
her pregnant caldera gave birth,
and too soon what was born gave death
and choked all life on all the Earth.
  WE COULD HAVE LIVED! In other words,
  we could have listened to the nerds.

This tale I have no wish to tell,
yet is true. It is not wrong.
If we do not start to dwell
above the sky, it won't be long
  before our children pay the cost
  and everyone we love is lost.

Michael rowed the boat ashore — *Allelujah*
Michael rowed the boat ashore — *Allelujah*

Henry pulled it up the ramp — *with the usual care*
Henry saw that it was damp — *and the wood was bare*

Timothy was standing by — *right beside it*
with a towel to make it dry — *and he dried it*

Tim revarnished all the wood — *with preservative*
Michael saw that it was good — *and superlative*

Michael asked if it was dear — *and expensive*
to stick a motor on the rear — *Tim was pensive*

Timothy said, "Twenty three — *hundred dollar"*
Michael said, "OK", 'cause he — *was a scholar*

Mike gave Timothy the cash — *every fiver*
Tim said Mike was very flash — *for a skiver*

Tim and Henry did a blitz — *worked in rota*
till the boat was done with its — *outboard motor*

Then they placed it in the sea — *nice and steady*
Michael said to Timothy, — *"Is it ready?"*

Tim said, "Yes", and pulled the cord — *just a fraction*
and the outboard motor roared — *into action*

Michael went off like a dart — *very fast was he*
Then the motor blew apart — *Mike was all at sea*

Tim and Henry couldn't ring — *for assistance*
Then young Henry saw a thing — *in the distance*

Do you know what Henry saw? — *Do ya? Do ya?*
Michael rowing for the shore — *Allelujah*

Michael rowed the boat ashore — *Allelujah*
Michael rowed the boat ashore — *Allelujah*